Integrated 1 Mathematics

Problem Bank

The Problem Bank includes additional problem situations for use with each section of the student text and a unifying problem for each unit of the student text. Answers are provided following the unifying problem for Unit 10.

McDougal Littell/Houghton Mifflin

Evanston, Illinois

Boston   Dallas   Phoenix

ISBN: 0-395-69811-1

23456789 - BW - 98 97 96 95

Contents

Name _____ Date _____

Problem Set 1

For use after Section 1-4

1. The graph shows the five most popular breeds of dogs registered with the American Kennel Club in 1989 and 1990.

1-1

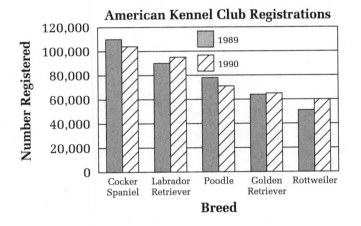

American Kennel Club Registrations

a. Which breeds were more popular in 1990 than in 1989? less popular?

b. What was the most popular breed of dog in 1989? in 1990?

c. What breed was about as popular in 1990 as it was in 1989?

2. Mrs. Davis worked out the budget for her family of five. She found that they spend $125 a week on groceries and $150 a month on clothing.

1-2

a. Write a variable expression for the amount spent on groceries in w weeks.

b. Write a variable expression for the amount spent on clothing in m months.

c. How much money does the Davis family spend on groceries and clothing in one year?

3. A female cat gives birth to an average of six female kittens each year. Suppose each female is neutered after it has produced six females.

1-3

a. The number of new female kittens born in year 1 is 6, in year 2 is 36, and so on. Write an expression for the number of new female kittens born in year x.

b. Use the expression from part (a) to calculate how many new females will be born in the 10th year.

4. Insert parentheses to make each statement true.

1-4

a. $30 \div 2 + 4 \times 2 + 7 = 10$

b. $30 \div 2 + 4 \times 2 + 7 = 51$

Problem Set 2

For use after Section 1-7

1. Edward Lennox gave a special exam for his math course. There were three sections of problems with 20 problems in each section. Problems in Section A were worth 5 points, problems in Section B were worth 7 points, and problems in Section C were worth 13 points. Each student could decide how many problems to do and from which sections. The variables *a, b,* and *c* tell how many problems a first student might have tried from sections A, B, and C, respectively. Suppose a second student tried exactly the problems that the first student did *not* work on.

   1-5

   a. Describe what the expression $5a + 7b + 13c$ represents.
   b. Describe what the expression $5(20 - a) + 7(20 - b) + 13(20 - c)$ represents.
   c. Use the distributive property to find the sum of the expressions in parts (a) and (b). How can you check your answer?

2. Draw a line through two dots on a piece of dot paper. Using dots on the paper as vertices, draw a polygon on one side of the line. Then, imagining that the line is a mirror, draw the polygon's reflection on the other side of the line. Are the two polygons congruent?

   1-6

3. What kind of movement (*flip, turn,* or *slide*) shows that the polygons in the figure are congruent?

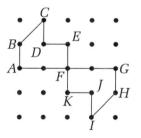

4. What name best describes each quadrilateral? Draw all lines of symmetry for each figure or write "no symmetry."

   1-7

   a.   **b.** a **c.**

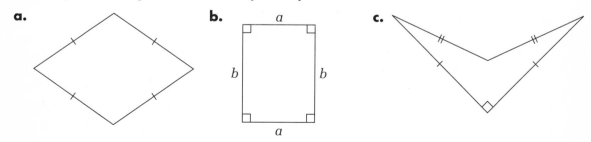

Name _____   Date _____

Unifying Problem 1

For use after Section 1-7

Refer to the figure below to answer the questions.

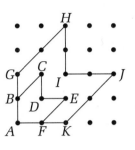

a. Are polygons *ABCDEF* and *AGHIJK* congruent?

b. Let *a* represent the distance from *A* to *B* and let *b* represent the distance from *B* to *C*. Write a variable expression for the perimeter of the smaller polygon.

c. Notice how the lengths of the sides of the large and small polygons are related. Write a variable expression for the perimeter of the larger polygon using the variables from part (b).

d. Compare the variable expressions from parts (b) and (c). How are they similar? different?

e. Draw another polygon of the same shape but with each side three times as long as the related side of the small polygon in the figure shown above. What do you predict the perimeter will be?

Problem Set 3

For use after Section 2-3

1. The frequent flier program that Eli belongs to keeps track of the miles he has flown. Last month he was credited with 5222 miles for a round-trip flight between Boston and Los Angeles. This month he has had two round-trip flights between Boston and San Francisco. He estimates that these trips will add a little over 18,000 miles to his mileage total. Is this a reasonable estimate? Explain.   **2-1**

2. Marty's doctor has told him that less than 30% of the calories he consumes at each meal should come from fat. He consumes about 1000 calories per meal. The label on his favorite dessert says that 500 of its calories come from fat. Is this a good choice for dessert if he eats the whole dessert at one meal? Explain.

3. Jonita and Sarah agreed to share the cost of building a kite for their science class. Jonita paid for the fabric and Sarah paid for the spars and other hardware. The total cost of the kite was $17.29. If the hardware cost $8.76, what was the cost of the fabric?   **2-2**

4. Tell whether the following statement is *true* or *false*. Explain.   **2-3**

$$2.6 \times 10^{27} + 3.2 \times 10^{27} = 5.8 \times 10^{27}$$

5. The mass of an atom is approximately the sum of the masses of its protons and neutrons. The mass of a proton is about 1.673×10^{-27} kg. The mass of a neutron is about 1.675×10^{-27} kg. Use this information for the following questions. Write each answer in scientific notation, with each decimal part rounded to the nearest thousandth.

   a. An oxygen atom has 8 protons and 8 neutrons in its nucleus. Estimate the mass of the oxygen atom.

   b. A sulfur atom has 16 protons and 16 neutrons in its nucleus. Estimate the mass of the sulfur atom.

   c. A chromium atom has 24 protons and 28 neutrons in its nucleus. Estimate the mass of the chromium atom.

Name _____ Date _____

Problem Set 4

For use after Section 2-6

1. Refer to the information about metric and customary units on page 79 of Unit 2. Julie is an average walker. It takes her about 20 min to walk to Tam's apartment and about 24 min to walk to the park. It is twice as far from Tam's apartment to the park as from Julie's house to Tam's apartment.

2-4

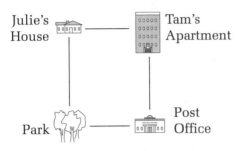

Julie's House — Tam's Apartment

Park — Post Office

   a. About how far is it from Julie's house to Tam's apartment in customary units?

   b. About how far is it from Julie's house to the park in metric units?

   c. About how long does it take Julie to walk to the park if she picks up Tam at his apartment on the way?

2. Find the measure of the third angle in each triangle. You may find it helpful to make a sketch for each situation.

2-5

   a. In triangle *DEF*, $\angle D = 81°$ and $\angle F = 76°$. Find the measure of $\angle E$.

   b. Triangle *JKL* is a right triangle. The measure of $\angle J$ is $16°$ and $\angle K$ is the right angle. Find the measure of $\angle L$.

3. The concession stand at Grand Football Stadium measures 15 ft long, 12 ft wide, and $9\frac{1}{2}$ ft high. The volume of the announcer's booth is 1900 ft³. Is the volume of the concession stand *greater than* or *less than* the volume of the announcer's booth? Explain.

2-6

4. The figure shows a rectangular box. Write and simplify an expression for each of the following.

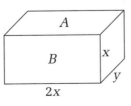

A

B   *x*

y

2x

   a. the area of the face marked *A*

   b. the area of the face marked *B*

   c. the volume of the box

Problem Set 5

For use after Section 2-9

━━━━━━━━━━━━━

For questions 1–4, write and solve an equation to find the unknown value.

1. Marisa jogged 1 mile to City Park. Then she jogged three times around the park. After jogging home she calculated that she had covered a total of 8 miles. What is the distance around City Park?

2-7

2. Jared wrapped 4 small gifts, all the same size, and 1 large gift. The large gift required 2 m of ribbon. Jared used 4 m of ribbon in all. How much ribbon did he use for each small gift?

3. Eight computer memory chips and a chip insertion tool cost $178.91. The price of the insertion tool is $6.99. Find the price of one chip.

2-8

4. Cherie had $8.50 and Kelli had $7.25 to spend at the carnival. Together they bought 12 ride tickets and had $.75 left over. How much did each ride ticket cost?

5. Baltazar is interested in finding out how the square root of a number compares with the cube root of the number.

2-9

    a. Is $\sqrt{481}$ *greater than* or *less than* $\sqrt[3]{481}$?

    b. If $x > 1$, is $\sqrt{x}$ *greater than* or *less than* $\sqrt[3]{x}$? Choose a value of x to support your answer.

    c. If $0 < x < 1$, is $\sqrt{x}$ *greater than* or *less than* $\sqrt[3]{x}$? Choose a value of x to support your answer.

6. The planet Pluto has a volume of about 35,000,000,000 mi^3. Imagine a cube with the same volume as Pluto. What would be the length of a side of the cube?

Unifying Problem 2

For use after Section 2-9

The City Council commissioned a concrete sculpture to be placed in the courtyard in front of City Hall. The figure shows the plans for the work. The small square will be paved with 81 ft^2 of stone and the large square will be paved with 144 ft^2 of brick. There will be a continuous bench along the perimeter of the inner triangle. The bench will measure 36 ft.

a. How many cubic feet of concrete will be needed to form the cube?

b. Suppose the Council will only pay for one-eighth as much concrete as calculated in part (a). What will be the revised areas of the small square and large square?

c. Refer to part (b). What will be the length of the new bench?

Problem Set 6

For use after Section 3-3

1. The matrix and graph both show recommended daily allowances (RDA) of three minerals for females.

3-1

Age	1	3	6	10	14	18	24
Folate	35	50	75	100	150	180	180
Iodine	50	70	90	120	150	150	150
Selenium	15	20	20	30	45	50	55

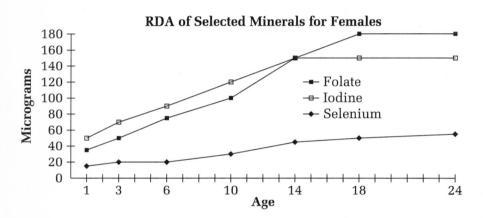

RDA of Selected Minerals for Females

a. What is the RDA of iodine for a 10-year-old girl?

b. Which nutrient has the greatest RDA increase with age?

c. For what age range is the RDA for iodine greater than that for folate?

d. What is the difference in the number of micrograms of selenium required by a 1-year-old and the number required by a 24-year-old?

e. For which mineral is the RDA consistently less than the RDA for other minerals?

2. Chip is on his school's golf team. He says his average for the last 9 games is 75 strokes. His best game was a 70 and his worst was 85. He most often completes the course in 74 strokes.

3-2

a. What are the mean, mode, and range of Chip's scores? Do you think that his 85 score is an outlier?

b. There is one game left for this season. What score does Chip need on his next game if he wants his average to be 74?

c. Can Chip lower his average score to 67? Explain.

3. For each mineral in Problem 1, write an inequality to describe the range in which the RDAs fall.

3-3

Problem Set 7

For use after Section 3-7

1. The Transportation Department wanted to know if there were enough toll booths at the entrance to a local turnpike. Each morning for a month they recorded the number of cars waiting in line at 7:30 A.M. The data they collected are shown below. Make a stem-and-leaf plot of these data.

3-4

    25, 10, 32, 42, 16, 27, 38, 19, 33, 24, 26, 19, 40, 36, 31
    14, 28, 31, 22, 15, 30, 26, 14, 29, 43, 20, 17, 15, 28, 35

2. The chart shows the number of sit-ups the students in two gym classes were able to do.

3-5

7:30 A.M.	10, 18, 24, 25, 30, 28, 31, 25, 32, 32, 33, 33, 41, 38, 44, 45, 38, 30, 31, 30, 23, 24, 19, 45, 43, 31, 32, 33
8:30 A.M.	10, 29, 34, 40, 37, 31, 28, 28, 30, 36, 41, 31, 29, 10, 29, 29, 37, 44, 45, 42, 30, 38, 25, 12, 12, 31, 41, 39

    a. Find the median, the mean, the high and low values, and the range for each class.

    b. Make a box-and-whisker plot for each class. Based on these plots, how would you compare the performance of the two classes?

3. The Kingston High Bugle is running a story about student dating habits. The journalists have circulated a survey asking students how often they go out on a date, where they like to go, and whether they go alone, with another couple, or with a larger group. What kind of graph is a good choice to display the data about the frequency of dating? favorite dating places? percentage of students going out with a group, doubles, or alone?

3-6

4. The chart shows the attendance at North Face Ski Resort (in thousands).

3-7

FALL	WINTER		SPRING	
Nov.	Dec.	Jan.	Feb.	Mar.	Apr.
15	43	50	45	32	10

    a. Draw a histogram with two-month intervals. Draw another histogram with the intervals Fall, Winter, Spring.

    b. A brochure advertising the resort said, "If you can't come in the off-season, it may be ten times as hard to get accommodations." Which graph do you think the brochure writer used? Do you consider the statement accurate? Why?

Unifying Problem 3

For use after Section 3-7

For the activity in this problem, you will need four dice.

a. Roll four dice 50 times. For each roll, record the total that the dice showed.

b. Make a stem-and-leaf plot of your data.

c. Make a frequency table with smaller intervals than your stem-and-leaf plot.

d. Make a histogram with the same intervals as your frequency table.

e. Which bars in your histogram are the longest? Why do you think this is so?

f. If you were to roll the four dice one more time, in which interval(s) do you think the total is most likely to fall?

g. Make a box-and-whisker plot of your data.

h. Suppose you were to repeat this activity with five dice. Which interval(s) do you think would have the most data in them? What do you think the median, the high and low, and quartiles would be? Draw a box-and-whisker plot based on your predictions.

Name _____ Date _____

Problem Set 8

For use after Section 4-4

1. Xavier and Dolores saved for years to go on a trip around the world. They started from their home in Mexico City, Mexico (20° N, 100° W). Use a globe or a world map to fill in the information on their itinerary.

Destination City/Country	Coordinates
Rio de Janeiro, Brazil	?
?	34°S, 18°E
Cairo, Egypt	?
?	49°N, 2°E
?	19°N, 73°E
Tokyo, Japan	?
?	38°N, 123°W
?	20°N, 100°W

4-1

2. Polygon *ABCD* has vertices *A*(2, 2), *B*(3, 5), *C*(5, 4), and *D*(5, 1).

4-2

   a. Draw *ABCD* on a coordinate grid.

   b. Take the opposite of the second coordinate of each point but keep the first coordinate the same. Graph the new figure.

   c. Predict what will happen to the original figure if you take the opposite of each first coordinate. Test your prediction.

3. Earl and Vanessa needed to make a geometric design for their art class. Vanessa suggested using graph paper with a coordinate grid marked on it to help them. Earl designed a parallelogram with vertices (–6, 3), (–2, 3), (0, 0), and (–4, 0). They translated this figure four units to the right. Then they translated the second figure two units right and three units down. Finally, they translated the third figure four units to the left. What are the coordinates of the vertices of each of these new figures? What figure is formed by the four parallelograms put together?

4-3

4. Use the letters on the outside of the gear to state where *A* is after each rotation around point *O*.

4-4

   a. 60° counterclockwise

   b. 60° clockwise

   c. 180° counterclockwise

   d. 240° counterclockwise

   e. Describe the rotational symmetry of the gear.

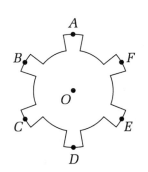

Problem Bank, INTEGRATED MATHEMATICS 1

Problem Set 9

For use after Section 4-7

---

1. Refer to the table at the right.

Miniature TV Sets	
List Price ($)	**Quality Rating**
600	86
550	75
650	70
450	51
300	50
369	48
300	40

4-5

    a. What kind of correlation, if any, do you think there is between the price and the quality rating of the miniature television sets? Why?

    b. Make a scatter plot of the data.

    c. Describe the correlation shown by the scatter plot. Does your scatter plot support your prediction from part (a)?

    d. Draw a fitted line on your scatter plot. What would you expect a miniature TV set with a quality rating of 60 to cost?

2. Describe each situation using the phrase "is a function of." What is the dependent variable? the control variable? Sketch how you think the graph might look.

4-6

    a. Once a week, Vinny withdraws $10 from his savings account. He starts with $120 in the account and never deposits any money.

    b. A video store manager records the number of tapes that are rented during each hour of the day. After collecting data for one week, the manager sees that the number of rentals is greatest in the evenings.

3. Write each function as an equation. Then graph the function.

4-7

    a. The cost of material bought at $4 per yard depends on the number of yards of material bought.

    b. Anthony types an average of 50 words per minute. The time he takes to type a report depends on the number of words the report contains.

4. In a right triangle, the two acute angles are complementary. Let x and y be the measures of these two acute angles.

    a. Describe the relationship between x and y.

    b. Make a table of values.

    c. Write an equation that represents the relationship.

    d. Graph the equation.

    e. What basic shape does this graph have?

    f. In which quadrant(s) are the points that represent the measures of the two acute angles? Explain.

Unifying Problem 4

For use after Section 4-7

A manufacturer of refrigeration equipment studied its competitors to learn how consumers rated the performance of different makes of ice chests.

a. The following table shows how a consumer focus group rated the ability of different makes of ice chests to keep contents cold. Ice chests that kept contents cold longer received higher ratings.

	A	B	C	D	E	F	G	H	I	J	K	L
Capacity (qt)	15.5	15.5	16.75	15.5	13.5	13.5	8.25	10.75	7.5	6.75	6.5	6.75
Cold-Keeping Rating	99	90	85	72	69	56	57	56	53	36	35	35

Make a scatter plot of the data and draw a fitted line. What cold-keeping rating would you predict for a 14-qt ice chest?

b. In part (a), you saw that ice chests with greater capacity usually have higher cold-keeping ratings that those with smaller capacity. This is due in part to the ratio of the ice chests' surface area to its capacity (volume). The ratio of surface area to volume is the value of $\frac{\text{surface area}}{\text{volume}}$. Copy the following table, which shows how the ratio of surface area to volume changes for a cube as the length of the edge increases. Extend the table to include edge lengths of 4, 5, 6, 7, and 8 units.

Edge Length (s)	Area of One Face (s^2)	Total Surface Area	Volume (s^3)	$\dfrac{\text{Surface Area}}{\text{Volume}}$
1	$1^2 = 1$	$6 \cdot 1 = 6$	$1^3 = 1$	$\dfrac{6}{1} = 6$
2	$2^2 = 4$	$6 \cdot 4 = 24$	$2^3 = 8$	$\dfrac{24}{8} = 3$
3	$3^2 = 9$	$6 \cdot 9 = 54$	$3^3 = 27$	$\dfrac{54}{27} = 2$

c. How does the ratio of surface area to volume change as the cubes get larger?

d. The ratio of surface area to volume is a function of edge length. Graph the function using the data in your table.

e. An ice chest is not necessarily shaped like a cube. What do you think you would observe if you found surface area to volume ratios for other shapes?

f. What factors other than the surface area to volume ratio might affect how well an ice chest keeps its contents cold?

Problem Set 10

For use after Section 5-4

1. A store sells about 70 CD players in a typical week. If they have a sale, they sell about 6 more CD players a week for every 5% they take off the current price.

    a. Model this situation for 0%, 5%, 10%, ... , 35%, 40% using a table or graph.

    b. If the store wants to sell at least 110 CD players in one week, what percent sale should they advertise in the paper?

        5-1

2. The rules for scoring Shannon and Dakota's biology test were the following:
Correct: +5 points, Incorrect: −5 points, No answer: 0 points

    a. There were 20 problems on the test and Dakota answered all of them. How many correct answers did he get if his total score was 80 points?

    b. Shannon wasn't sure on three questions, so she left them blank. How many correct answers did she get if her total score was 75 points?

        5-2

3. Meilei and her grandfather are having a race. Meilei estimates that she can run at a rate of 300 m/min and her grandfather can run at a rate of 250 m/min.

    a. How far can each run in 5 min? in n min?

    b. Meilei lets her grandfather run for 1 min before she starts. Let t be the total time of the race in minutes. Using the variable t, write an expression for the distance that each runs.

    c. Suppose the race ends in a tie. How many minutes did the race take? What distance did it cover?

        5-3

4. Jennie and Alice live 16 km apart and agree to meet along Manning Street so that Jennie can borrow Alice's tape player. Alice walks 6 km/h and leaves after they hang up the phone. Jennie must clean her room before she can leave. She leaves 1 h later than Alice and rides her bike 14 km/h. Write an equation to represent this situation. Then solve the equation.

5. Solve this number puzzle and graph the solution on a number line: I am thinking of a number. Its opposite is greater than the difference you get when you subtract 72 from 5 times the number. What are the possible numbers that I could be thinking of?

        5-4

6. Marlena is making a quilt and needs 5 in.^{2} of fabric for each square plus 70 in.^{2} for the border. She has a scrap piece of fabric that is 150 in.^{2}. What is the maximum number of squares she can make without having to buy more fabric?

Name _____ Date _____

Problem Set 11

For use after Section 5-8

1. Karlita has $18 to buy tickets for her relatives to attend the school play. Student tickets cost $2 and adult tickets cost $3.

    a. Model the situation with an equation.

    b. Rewrite the equation to show the number of adult tickets, a, Karlita can buy if she buys s student tickets.

    c. If Karlita buys 6 student tickets, how many adult tickets can she buy?

    5-5

2. When a substance contains no heat energy, its temperature is called *absolute zero*. The Kelvin (K) scale and the Rankine (R) scale use absolute zero as their starting points. The formula

    $$R = \frac{9}{5}K$$

    relates temperatures on these scales.

    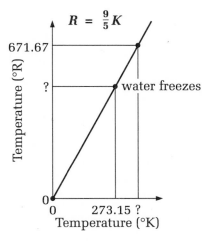

    5-6

    a. Solve the formula for K.

    b. Find the Rankine temperature for 273.15°K. Check the reasonableness of your answer on the graph above.

    c. Find the Kelvin temperature for 671.67°R. Check the reasonableness of your answer on the graph above.

3. Sensei Takai is building a new dojo for his Karate school. The training floor will be shaped like a trapezoid with bases of 35 ft and 25 ft. The distance from the front to the back of the floor is 35 ft. If each student requires about 36 ft^2 to train, what is the greatest number of students Sensei Takai will be able to enroll in each class?

    5-7

4. Jorgen and Elisa went to the State Fair to go on the rides. Jorgen used 18 tickets to ride the roller coaster three times and the log flume twice. Elisa used 11 tickets to ride the roller coaster twice and the log flume once. How many tickets were needed for a ride on the roller coaster? the log flume?

    5-8

Unifying Problem 5

For use after Section 5-8

Refer to the following figure.

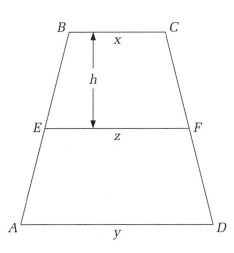

a. Draw a trapezoid like trapezoid *ABCD* in the figure. Draw the line segment *EF* that is parallel to the bases, connects the legs, and divides the altitude in half. Measure the lengths *x*, *y*, *z*, and *h*.

b. Draw two more trapezoids with the same values for *x* and *y* but with different altitudes. Does the value of *z* change with the altitude?

c. Write a variable expression for the area of trapezoid *ABCD*; trapezoid *AEFD*; trapezoid *EBCF*.

d. Using the variable expressions from part (c) write an equation showing the relationship between the area of the large trapezoid and the areas of the two smaller trapezoids.

e. Solve the equation in part (d) for *z*.

f. Does the equation in part (e) have the variable *h* in it? What does this tell you about the relationship of the length of line segment *EF* and the altitude of the large trapezoid?

g. What is the relationship between the length of line segment *EF* and the lengths of the bases of the large trapezoid?

Problem Set 12

For use after Section 6-3

For Problems 1 and 2, refer to the circle graph.

1. There were about 95,000,000 households in the United States in 1990. Find the number of households that had at least one television set. Show two different methods for solving the problem.

6-1

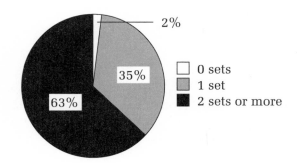

2%

☐ 0 sets
▨ 1 set
■ 2 sets or more

35%

63%

2. In 1990 in the United States, 56,072,270 households had cable television service. What percent of the households with at least one television received cable service?

3. Miriam put 20 playing cards into a bag. Oscar's experiment was to take a card out, record if it was a red or a black card, return it to the bag, and mix the cards up. He performed his experiment 5 times, recording 4 red cards and 1 black card.

6-2

  a. What was the experimental probability of pulling a red card out of the bag?

  b. Miriam told Oscar that she had put 10 red cards and 10 black cards into the bag. What was the theoretical probability of pulling a red card out of the bag?

  c. Do you think the answer for part (a) will change if Oscar performed his experiment 1000 times? Explain your answer.

4. The teachers in the Wylie School District are negotiating to reduce the pupil-teacher ratio from 30:1 to 25:1. There are 12,000 students in the district. If each additional teacher will cost the district $30,000, what will be the added costs to the district if the teachers are successful in the negotiations?

6-3

5. Last season, Babe Boggs had 240 hits in 600 times at bat. This season his batting average was the same, but he had only 500 official at-bats. How many hits did he have this season?

6. Suppose a bushel of apples makes slightly more than 3 gallons of cider. How many bushels of apples are needed to make 50 gallons of cider?

Problem Set 13

For use after Section 6-7

1. Falls City Council needed an estimate of the number of pigeons in the city. They hired a wildlife biologist who captured and tagged 50 pigeons. A month after the tagged pigeons were released, she captured another 50 pigeons and found that 5 of them were tagged.

   a. What is the biologist's estimate of the total number of pigeons in the city?

   b. If a second sample of 50 included 20 tagged birds, what would the new estimate be?

   c. Compare the estimates found in parts (a) and (b). What factors might cause such a big discrepancy in estimates?

   6-4

2. Peter Putnam is building a hill as part of his "N-gauge" model railroad layout. The scale of an N-gauge set is 1 in.:13 ft 4 in. Peter wants the model to represent a 250 ft hill. How many inches high should he make the model?

   6-5

3. The picture frame in the diagram has a width of 1 in. on all sides.

   a. What are the dimensions of the inner rectangle?

   b. Are the two rectangles similar? Why or why not?

   c. How could you draw a picture frame different from the one in the diagram so that the outer and inner rectangles are similar?

   6-6

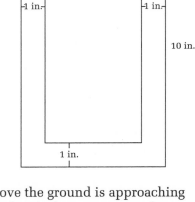

6 in.
1 in.
1 in.
1 in.
1 in.
10 in.

4. An airplane flying 30,000 feet above the ground is approaching an airport tower. One minute ago the airplane was spotted at an angle of 25°. Now the angle of the plane is 50°. Estimate the speed of the airplane in feet per minute and miles per hour.

   6-7

50°
25°
30,000 ft

Name _____ Date _____

Unifying Problem 6

For use after Section 6-7

The Floating Clouds Parachuting Club is doing a targeting demonstration
for the city's Founder's Day festival. They have laid out a 20 m by 20 m
square on the fair grounds, with a diamond drawn inside it, as shown in
the diagram. Assuming that the parachuters will land at random
positions within the square, what is the probability that a club member
will land inside the diamond? (*Hint:* Compare the areas of the square and
the diamond.)

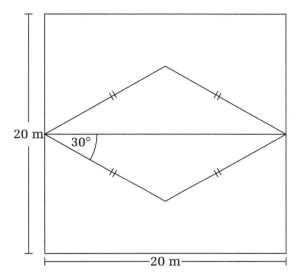

Problem Set 14

For use after Section 7-3

1. The cost of carpeting a room varies directly with the area of the room. For a certain brand of carpet, it costs $479.40 to cover 12 square yards.   **7-1**

   a. Write a direct variation equation that expresses this situation.

   b. Find the variation constant.

   c. Find the cost of carpeting 20 square yards.

   d. What factors may lead to different variation constants when buying carpet?

2. A ship is approaching a harbor at night. The navigator spots the lighthouse on the shore at an angle of elevation of 5.7°. The charts show that the light is 100 ft above sea level. How far is the ship from the shore?

3. Juanita drops a table tennis ball. Here are her results.   **7-2**

Drop height, D (in.)	Mean bounce height, B (in.)
12	5
24	11
36	16
48	20

   a. Plot these data on a graph and draw a fitted line.

   b. Find the slope of the line you have drawn. Explain how you calculated the slope.

   c. Suppose Juanita drops the table tennis ball from a height of 30 in. Use the graph to predict the bounce height.

4. Rex is a golden retriever whose owner has tied his leash to a large tree. The diameter of the tree is 2 ft. If Rex is left with 19 ft of leash, about how many times can he wrap the leash around the tree clockwise before he can no longer run in that direction?   **7-3**

5. A landscape architect is designing the border of a circular park with a diameter of 100 yards. She plans to plant maple trees around 120° of the circumference. If the trees are to be planted about 10 feet apart, how many trees will be planted?

Problem Set 15

For use after Section 7-6

1. Model each situation with a direct variation equation in general   **7-4**
form. Then use the equation to answer the question.

    a. A jet airliner maintains a constant speed and flies
3000 miles in 4 hours. How many miles does it fly in
2.5 hours?

    b. Berta can paint 100 tennis shoes in 5 days. How long does
it take her to paint 60 shoes?

    c. Doug paid $19.50 for 10 sections of track for his model
train. How much would he have to pay for 15 sections?

2. A telephone call costs 27.3 cents per minute. Find the rate in   **7-5**
cents per hour and then in dollars per hour.

3. On the day the Nguyen family left for Mexico, 1 U.S. dollar was
worth 3.12 pesos.

    a. If the Nguyen's bought 1250 U.S. dollars worth of pesos,
how many pesos did they buy?

    b. The Nguyen family paid 41.6 pesos for 32 liters of gasoline.
How many U.S. dollars per gallon did the Nguyen's pay for
the gasoline? (1 liter ≈ 0.26 gallons)

4. For this problem, refer to the following diagram, which shows   **7-6**
the layout of an athletic field.

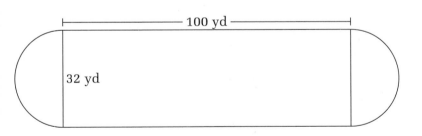

If the groundskeeper needs to apply a kilogram of fertilizer for
every 75 square yards of grass, about how many kilograms of
fertilizer are needed? (Assume that the ends of the field
are semicircles.)

5. A circular spinner with a diameter of 20 cm is divided into three
equal sectors. The sectors are labeled A, B, and C.

    a. What is the central angle of each sector?

    b. What is the area of each sector?

    c. What is the probability of the spinner stopping in
sector A? in sector B? in sector C?

Problem Bank, INTEGRATED MATHEMATICS 1

Unifying Problem 7

For use after Section 7-6

A square with side length *s* is drawn. A circle is drawn around the
square so that the circle intersects the square at its four corners. Another
circle is drawn inside the square so that the circle intersects the square at
the midpoints of its sides.

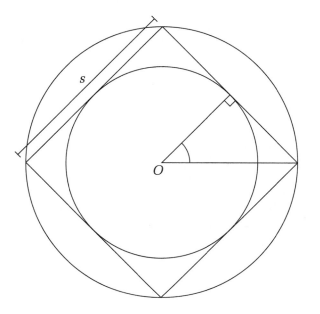

1. Find the radius, the circumference, and the area of the small
   circle in terms of *s*.

2. Find the radius, the circumference, and the area of the large
   circle in terms of *s*.
   (*Hint:* Use trigonometric ratios to find the sides of the triangle
   drawn in the figure.)

3. Write a direct variation equation to model each relationship.

   a. the circumference of the small circle and the perimeter of
      the square

   b. the circumference of the large circle and the perimeter of
      the square

   c. the circumferences of the two circles

   d. the area of the small circle and the area of the square

   e. the area of the large circle and the area of the square

   f. the areas of the two circles

4. Suppose you are given a circle and are asked to draw another
   circle whose area is exactly half of the area of the first circle.
   Using what you have learned from problems 1–3, how would
   you do it?

Name _____ Date _____

Problem Set 16

For use after Section 8-3

1. At the start of a race, Crispin is 400 m from the finish line. He runs at a constant rate of 8 m/s. His distance from the finish line is a function of the number of seconds since the race began. **8-1**

    a. Complete the table of values and graph the points.

seconds since the race began (s)	0	1	2	5	10	20
distance from the finish line (d)						

    b. Find the slope and the vertical intercept of the graph. How are they related to Crispin's distance from the finish line?

    c. Use the graph to predict when Crispin will cross the finish line. Tell what part of the graph you used.

    d. Write an equation for d in terms of s.

    e. Write an inequality to describe the numbers that can be used for s.

2. Jolene and Frank took turns stuffing 600 envelopes for their club's newsletter. It takes Jolene 10 minutes to stuff 60 envelopes. Frank can get 60 envelopes done in 12 minutes. **8-2**

    a. How many envelopes can Jolene stuff per minute? How many can Frank stuff per minute?

    b. Let j be the number of minutes that Jolene worked and let f be the number of minutes Frank worked. Write an equation in standard form relating j, f, and the total number of envelopes stuffed.

    c. Make a graph of the equation from part (b).

    d. Find the intercepts of the graph in part (c). What do they represent in this situation?

3. The charge for a group ski lesson is $100 for the group, regardless of how many students attend. Write an equation that models the relationship between the charge for the ski lesson and the number of students in the group. What is the slope of the graph of this equation? **8-3**

4. Kwan plotted the following points on a line graph: (−2, 3), (−2, 4), (−2, −1), and (−2, 0).

    a. What should his graph look like? What equation describes the graph?

    b. Kwan says that the slope of the graph is zero. Is he correct? Explain.

Problem Set 17

For use after Section 8-5

---

1. Between the ages of 1 and 7, children gain about the same amount of weight each year. At age 2, Andrea weighed 28 lb. At age 5, she weighed 40 lb.

    a. What are the control and dependent variables in this situation?

    b. Represent the given information as two points on a graph.

    c. Find the rate of Andrea's growth.

    d. Write an equation for Andrea's weight in terms of her age.

8-4

2. If a report is not turned in on time in Jonah's American history class, his teacher will deduct 10 points for each day it is late. Jonah turned in his last report 2 days late and received a score of 72.

    a. Write an equation for Jonah's score on the report as a function of the number of days it is late.

    b. What score would he have received had the report been on time?

3. A school theater group is holding a bake sale to raise money for a show. They plan to sell brownies and have already spent $5 on posters. Brownies cost $.30 each to make. The group sells each brownie for $.50.

    a. Write an equation for the expenses, using the number of brownies as the control variable.

    b. Write an equation for the income from the bake sale, using the number of brownies as the control variable.

    c. Graph the two equations on the same axes. Estimate the solution of the system of equations.

    d. The point of intersection is called the *break-even point*. What does it represent?

    e. Solve the system of equations by substitution.

    f. Suppose the theater group charges more for brownies. Choose a different price. Describe how this changes the number of brownies they have to sell to break even.

8-5

Problem Bank, INTEGRATED MATHEMATICS 1

Name _____ Date _____

Problem Set 18

For use after Section 8-7

1. Gabriella wants to earn money so she can sponsor a needy child.   **8-6**
Her parents pay her $5 an hour to do chores around the house
and she earns $3 an hour baby-sitting.

  a. Write a linear combination that expresses the amount of
  money she could earn in a month by spending c hours
  doing chores and b hours baby-sitting.

  b. Gabriella wants to contribute more than $50 a month for the
  child. Write a linear inequality that expresses this and
  graph the inequality.

2. A greenhouse owner is planning to plant two kinds of plants.
One seedling requires 50 mL of water per day and the other
requires 100 mL of water per day. There are only 150 L
(150,000 mL) of water available to the greenhouse for this
purpose each day. Write a linear inequality to express this
situation and graph it.

3. Emilie is sending some workbooks and second-hand textbooks to   **8-7**
an orphanage in Brazil. The workbooks weigh 1.5 lb each and
the textbooks weigh 5 lb each.

  a. The total shipping weight must not exceed 200 lb. Write a
  linear inequality to model this situation.

  b. Emilie wants each of the 50 orphans to have at least one
  book. Write an inequality to model this fact.

  c. Graph the system of inequalities. What is the greatest
  number of books Emilie can send? (*Note*: At least one
  textbook must be sent.)

4. A lever, such as a seesaw, is in balance when the weight on one
side of the fulcrum times its lever arm (the distance from the
weight to the point where the lever turns) equals the weight on
the other side times its lever arm. Maya and her little brother are
playing on a seesaw. Maya weighs 100 lb, her little brother
weighs 75 lb, and the length of the seesaw is 20 ft.

  a. Write an equation that models the situation when the
  seesaw is in balance.

  b. Suppose the seesaw is tipped toward Maya's brother. Write
  an inequality for this new situation.

  c. Maya's brother is sitting less than 2 feet farther from the
  fulcrum than Maya. Write an inequality modeling this
  relationship.

  d. Graph the system of two inequalities.

Unifying Problem 8

For use after Section 8-7

Mighty Good Nuts is making a new mix that will contain only peanuts and cashews. The sample batch will need to be at least 100 lb. The amount of peanuts must not exceed 3 times the amount of cashews. There are only 50 lb of cashews and 100 lb of peanuts available for this sample.

a. Write four inequalities to represent the four conditions that the sample must meet.

b. Graph the system of inequalities. What shape is the region that contains the solutions to the inequalities?

c. What are the coordinates of the points that are the vertices of the polygon from part (b)?

d. Peanuts cost $1.79 per lb, and cashews cost $3.99 per lb. Write a linear expression that represents the cost of preparing this sample.

e. Mathematicians can prove that in a case such as this the minimum cost will occur at one of the vertices of the polygon you found in part (c). Which combination of peanuts and cashews will cost the least to prepare? How much will it cost?

Problem Set 19

For use after Section 9-3

1. Mika is making a banner by sewing ribbon to a felt background, as shown in the figure. She'll use 18 in. lengths of ribbon for the top and bottom, and 12 in. lengths for the sides. Then she will sew two lengths of ribbon diagonally to make the cross. About how much ribbon will she need in all?

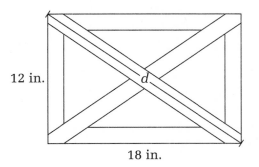

12 in.

d

18 in.

9-1

2. West Pondville is 8 mi due west of Pondville Center and North Pondville is 10 mi due north of Pondville Center. How far is it from West Pondville to North Pondville? Express your answer in simplified radical form.

9-2

3. Joey told his cousin, "All the girls I date go to West High." Write this statement as an "if-then" statement. Write the converse of his statement. Do you think the converse is true?

9-3

4. Floyd is buying a new home and wants to make sure that the home is "square," that is, that the walls make right angles with the floors and with each other. He makes three triangles, as shown in the figure, and measures the lengths of their sides. Are the walls "square" with each other? with the floor? Explain.

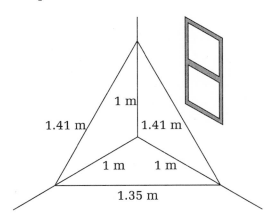

1 m

1.41 m

1.41 m

1 m   1 m

1.35 m

Problem Set 20

For use after Section 9-6

1. Lars lives near an airport. He has observed that from the time it first comes in view, it takes the average airplane about 10 min to reach the airport. There are about 20 flights a day. What is the probability that Lars will see an airplane when he picks a random time to go out into his yard?

9-4

2. Design a spinner with red, green, and blue areas, so that the probability of the spinner pointing to red, green, and blue is $\frac{1}{12}, \frac{3}{4},$ and $\frac{1}{6},$ respectively. What are the central angles of each sector?

3. The Glenview High Science Club is preparing their display for the All-State Science Fair. They have a 5 ft by 5 ft booth with walls 7 ft high. They want to add a roof to make their booth 10 ft high in the middle, but have a limited amount of fabric to use as a cover. Raoul wants to make the roof in the shape of a triangular prism, but Sue prefers a square pyramid. The club decided to choose the design which required the least amount of fabric. Which design did they choose? If the fabric also covers three sides of the booth, how much fabric is needed in all?

9-5

4. The Turner Plastics Company needs to make a cast aluminum mold for one of their products. The specifications for the mold are shown in the figure. The curved edges at the front and rear are half circles. How many cubic centimeters of aluminum will be needed?

9-6

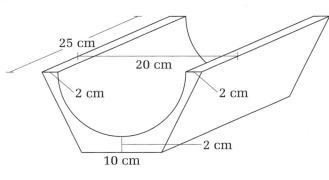

Name _____ Date _____

Problem Set 21

For use after Section 9-8

1. The poetry club plans to sell homemade ice cream served in   **9-7**
    waffles at the school carnival. They have to choose between a
    style of waffle that can be rolled into a perfect cone, or one
    which can be bent into a square pyramid. If the diameter of the
    base of the cone is the same length as a side of the base of the
    pyramid and they both have the same depth, which style will
    hold the most ice cream?

2. Mrs. Theissen used an overhead projector to enlarge a table of   **9-8**
    data 500% for her chemistry class. (That is, the dimensions of
    the table were increased by a factor of 5.) The original table
    measured 5 in. by 7 in. By what factor was the area enlarged?
    What was the area of the enlarged table?

3. The Tridex Company plans to build a new warehouse exactly
    like the one it now has but with a storage capacity 8 times
    greater. The current warehouse is 300 ft long and has the shape
    of a rectangular box.

    a. How long will the new warehouse be?
    b. If the current warehouse is 100 ft wide and 40 ft high, what
            is its capacity in cubic feet?
    c. What will be the capacity of the new warehouse if its width
            and height are the same as the current warehouse?

Unifying Problem 9

For use after Section 9-8

1. The drawing shows five squares with sides of length 1, *a*, *b*, *c*, and *d*.

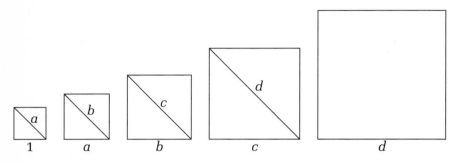

a. Find the lengths *a*, *b*, *c*, and *d* in simplified form.

b. Using the values you found for *a*, *b*, *c*, and *d*, describe the pattern.

c. Predict the length *e*, the hypotenuse of a right triangle whose legs have length *d*.

d. What is the area of each square?

e. Using the values for the areas of the squares, describe the pattern.

f. Predict the area of the next square in the pattern.

2. The figure shows a cube with edges of length 1.

a. Find the length of the diagonal $\overline{AB}$.

b. Suppose you constructed a cube with edges of length *AB*. What would be the length of a diagonal of this new cube?

c. Predict the lengths of the diagonals of the next 3 cubes in the pattern.

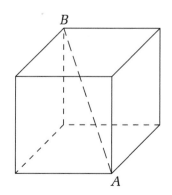

Problem Set 22

For use after Section 10-3

---

1. Solve Pia's puzzle. *I drew a triangle and a line of reflection through the triangle. When I reflected the triangle over the line, it reflected onto itself. What kind of triangle did I draw? Describe the line of reflection.*

   10-1

2. Each diagram shows a figure and its image. What is the line of reflection?

   a. 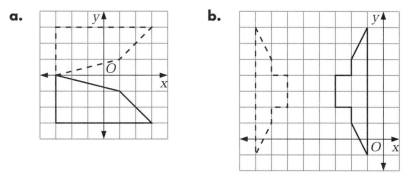   **b.**

3. Lucas wondered if he could find a parabola that would go through any three points he picked. He picked three points at random, plotted them on graph paper, and tried to sketch a parabola that would contain all three points.

   10-2

   a. Do you think there is a parabola that contains all three of the points that Lucas selected? Explain your thinking.

   b. Is it possible to find a parabola containing all three of the points (4, 7), (10, 7), and (12, 7)? Explain your thinking.

4. When Ayita entered a function on her graphics calculator, she got this graph.

   10-3

   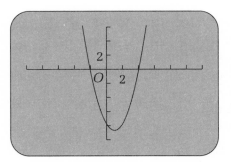

   a. Write the function for Ayita's graph. Here is a hint: The equation looks like $y = (x + \underline{\ ?\ })(x - \underline{\ ?\ })$.

   b. Graph the equation you wrote in part (a). Does your graph look like Ayita's? If not, try another guess.

Problem Set 23

For use after Section 10-6

1. Diedre and Matt did their math homework separately, then they compared their answers. For each problem, who has the correct answer? What do you think was the other's mistake?

10-4

		Diedre's Answer	Matt's Answer
a.	$(x^2y)^3$	x^6y^3	x^5y^3
b.	$(3b)^2$	$3b^2$	$9b^2$
c.	$(-k^2)^5$	k^{10}	$-k^{10}$

2. Marshall was hired to move packing boxes from one office to another. He needed to calculate the volume the boxes would take up in his truck. He did not have a tape measure with him, so he used a short length of rope. All the boxes were identical cubes with edges measuring 3 rope lengths.

   a. Using the variable r to represent each rope length, write an expression for the volume of each box.

   b. Marshall measured the inside of his truck and found it to be 9 by 12 by 6 rope lengths. Write a variable expression for the available volume in Marshall's truck.

   c. How many boxes will Marshall be able to take in one trip?

3. The figure shows the quilt panel Marietta designed. She chose a side length, s, for each square, and she cut each of the other rectangles s units long and 1 unit wide.

10-5

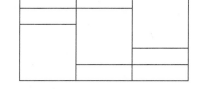

   a. Write a variable expression for the area of the panel.

   b. To complete her quilt, Marietta will have to sew a solid-color rectangle to the back of the panel. Factor the expression from part (a). Does the factored form show the dimensions of the solid-color rectangle?

4. Write an equation (in factored form) for a parabola that has the given x-intercepts.

   a. 3, 5   **b.** −1, 4   **c.** −10, −20

5. The product $(x + 2)(x - 3)$ is of the form $(x + n)(x + m)$, where n and m are positive or negative integers. When you expand a product of this form, do you think the result is always a trinomial? If not, give a counterexample.

10-6

Problem Set 24

For use after Section 10-8

1. Antoine is factoring a trinomial with a constant term of −24.   **10-7**

   a. Make a table showing the combinations of two factors he can try to get −24.

   b. Will the number of combinations be different if the constant term is 24? Explain.

Match each graph with the correct equation. Then explain how you decided which graph matched each equation.

2. $y = (x + 1)(x + 2)$ 3. $y = (x + 1)(x - 2)$

4. $y = x^2 + x - 2$ 5. $y = x^2 - 3x + 2$

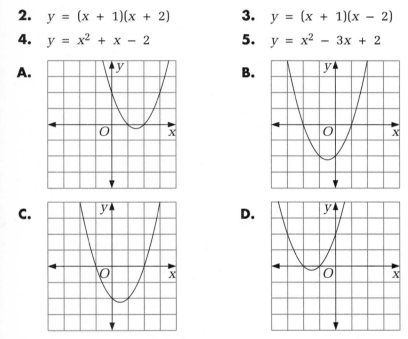

A.   B.

C.   D.

6. Morris High School's Physics club shot a model rocket off a   **10-8**
   100 m cliff. The flight of a projectile launched at 40 m/sec
   at 45°, from a height of 100 m, can be modeled by the equation
   $y = -4.9x^2 + 28.3x + 100$, where x represents the number of
   seconds from launch and y is the height in meters of the
   projectile above the ground.

   a. Find the y-intercept of this function. What does this represent in the situation?

   b. Use the quadratic formula to find the zeroes of this function. Which zero is irrelevant to the situation? What does the other zero represent?

   c. What height did the projectile reach?

Unifying Problem 10

For use after Section 10-8

---

1. On the same axes, draw the graphs of each of the following equations. Use a graphics calculator if you prefer.

   a. $y = x^2$

   b. $y = x^2 + 2x - 1$

   c. $y = x^2 + 3x - 1$

   d. $y = x^2 + 4x - 1$

   e. $y = x^2 + 5x - 1$

   f. $y = x^2 + 6x - 1$

   g. What is the effect of increasing the coefficient of x?

   h. What do you predict would happen if the coefficients of x were negative?

2. Consider the graphs you drew in parts (b)–(f) of Problem 1. Do all of these graphs have the same shape as the graph of $y = x^2$? Describe a method that would let you decide algebraically whether the curves do or do not have the same shape.

Answers

Problem Set 1

1.a. Labrador Retrievers, Golden Retrievers, and Rottweilers; Cocker Spaniels and Poodles   **b.** Cocker Spaniels; Cocker Spaniels   **c.** Golden Retrievers
2.a. $125w$ **b.** $150m$ **c.** $8300   **3.a.** 6^x
b. 60,466,176   **4.a.** $30 \div (2 + 4 \times 2) + 7 = 10$
b. $30 \div 2 + 4 \times (2 + 7) = 51$

Problem Set 2

1.a. the score of the first student if all problems attempted are correct   **b.** the score of the second student if all problems attempted are correct
c. $5a + 7b + 13c + 5(20 - a) + 7(20 - b) + 13(20 - c) = 5a + 7b + 13c + 100 - 5a + 140 - 7b + 260 - 13c = 500$; The maximum possible score is $5 \cdot 20 + 7 \cdot 20 + 13 \cdot 20 = 500$.
2. For drawings, check students' work. Yes.   **3.** turn

4.a.   rhombus;

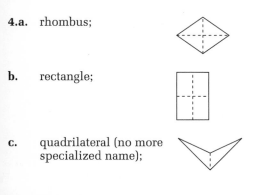

b.   rectangle;

c.   quadrilateral (no more specialized name);

Unifying Problem 1

1.a. No.   **b.** $4a + 2b$ **c.** $8a + 4b$ **d.** The two expressions have the same variables. The coefficients of the second expression are twice the coefficients of the first expression.

e.

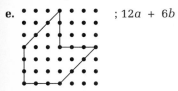   ; $12a + 6b$

Problem Set 3

1. The estimate is not reasonable. It is about as far from Boston to Los Angeles as from Boston to San Francisco, so two round trips between Boston and Los Angeles should give him about 10,500 or 11,000 miles.
2. No. 500 is 50% of 1000.   **3.** $8.53   **4.** True; The sum equals $(2.6 + 3.2) \times 10^{27}$.
5.a. 2.678×10^{-26} kg   **b.** 5.357×10^{-26} kg
c. 8.705×10^{-26} kg

Problem Set 4

1.a. about 1 mi   **b.** about 2 km   **c.** about 1 hour
2.a. $23°$ **b.** $74°$ **3.** less than; $1710 \text{ ft}^3 < 1900 \text{ ft}^3$
4.a. $2xy$ **b.** $2x^2$ **c.** $2x^2y$

Problem Set 5

1. $3d + 2 = 8$; 2 mi   **2.** $4r + 2 = 4$; 0.5 m
3. $8c + 6.99 = 178.91$; $21.49
4. $8.50 + 7.25 - 12t = 0.75$; $1.25   **5.a.** greater than   **b.** greater than; Answers may vary. An example is given. $x = 481$ **c.** less than; Answers may vary. An example is given. $x = 0.64$ **6.** about 3271 mi

Unifying Problem 2

1.a. 3375 ft^3 **b.** 20.25 ft^2; 36 ft^2 **c.** 18 ft

Problem Set 6

1.a. 120 micrograms   **b.** folate   **c.** from age 1 up to 14   **d.** 40 micrograms   **e.** selenium   **2.a.** 75; 74; 15; Yes.   **b.** 65   **c.** No. Chip would have to have a negative score on his last game in order to have a 67 average.   **3.** folate: $35 \le f \le 180$; iodine: $50 \le i \le 150$; selenium: $15 \le s \le 55$

Problem Set 7

1.

1	0 4 4 5 5 6 7 9 9
2	0 2 4 5 6 6 7 8 8 9
3	0 1 1 2 3 5 6 8
4	0 2 3

2.a. 31, 31, 10, 45, 35; 31, 31, 10, 45, 35

b.

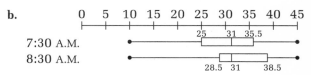

The 8:30 A.M. class has higher quartiles. Students in the 8:30 A.M. class performed slightly better than the 7:30 A.M. students.

3. histogram; bar graph; circle graph

4.a.

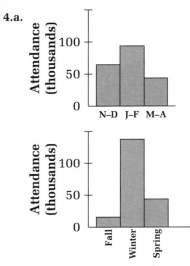

b. The brochure writer probably used the season histogram. No. The season histogram gives the impression that in each month of the winter season, bookings are ten times greater than in November, and this is *not* true.

Unifying Problem 3

a–d. Check students' work.   **e.** bars for the middle intervals; There are more possible combinations that give these totals.   **f.** one of the middle intervals
g. Check students' work.   **h.** the middle intervals; 17.5, 5, 30, 15, 20; For box-and-whisker plots, check students' work.

Problem Set 8

Coordinates may vary. Examples are given.

1.

Destination City/Country	Coordinates
Rio de Janeiro, Brazil	23°S, 43°W
Cape Town, South Africa	34°S, 18°E
Cairo, Egypt	30°N, 32°E
Paris, France	49°N, 2°E
Bombay, India	19°N, 73°E
Tokyo, Japan	36°N, 140°E
San Francisco, U.S.A.	38°N, 123°W
Mexico City, Mexico	20°N, 100°W

2.a–b.

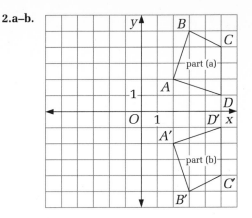

c. The figure will be flipped over the vertical axis.
3. second figure: (−2, 3), (2, 3), (4, 0), (0, 0); third figure: (0, 0), (4, 0), (6, −3), (2, −3); fourth figure: (−4, 0), (0, 0), (2, −3), (−2, −3); a parallelogram   **4.a.** *B*
b. *F*   **c.** *D*   **d.** *E*   **e.** The gear has 60°, 120°, 180°, 240°, and 300° rotational symmetry.

Problem Set 9

1.a. positive correlation; For the most part, the higher the price, the higher the quality rating.
b–d.

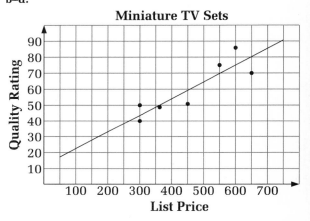

c. positive correlation; Yes.   **d.** Answers may vary. An example is given. $460   **2.a.** The balance in Vinny's account is a function of the number of weeks since the time his balance was $120. the balance in the account; the number of weeks; Sketches may vary. An example is given.

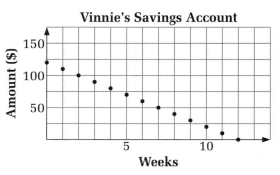

b. The number of tapes rented is a function of the time of day. number of tapes; time of day; Sketches may vary. An example is given.

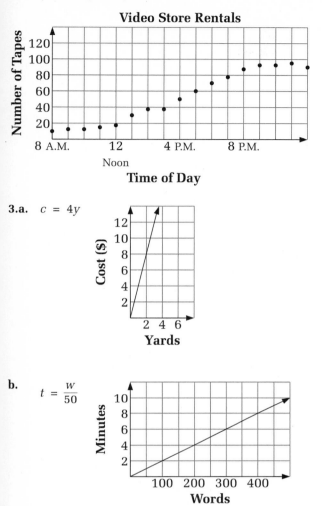

3.a. $c = 4y$

b. $t = \dfrac{w}{50}$

4.a. The sum of the measures of the acute angles is 90°. **b.** Answers may vary. An example is given.

x	y
20	70
40	50
60	30
80	10

c. $x + y = 90$

d.

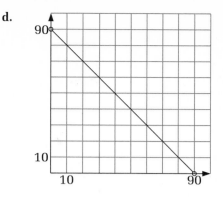

e. The graph for the equation is a line, but only the part in quadrant I is appropriate for the situation.
f. quadrant I; The measure of an angle must be positive.

Unifying Problem 4

a.

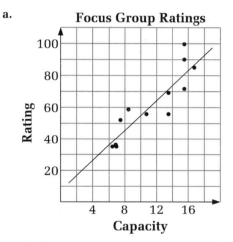

Predictions may vary. An example is given. 75

---

b.

Edge Length (s)	Area of One Face (s^2)	Total Surface Area	Volume (s^3)	$\frac{\text{Surface Area}}{\text{Volume}}$
1	$1^2 = 1$	$6 \cdot 1 = 6$	$1^3 = 1$	$\frac{6}{1} = 6$
2	$2^2 = 4$	$6 \cdot 4 = 24$	$2^3 = 8$	$\frac{24}{8} = 3$
3	$3^2 = 9$	$6 \cdot 9 = 54$	$3^3 = 27$	$\frac{54}{27} = 2$
4	$4^2 = 16$	$6 \cdot 16 = 96$	$4^3 = 64$	$\frac{96}{64} = 1.5$
5	$5^2 = 25$	$6 \cdot 25 = 150$	$5^3 = 125$	$\frac{150}{125} = 1.2$
6	$6^2 = 36$	$6 \cdot 36 = 216$	$6^3 = 216$	$\frac{216}{216} = 1$
7	$7^2 = 49$	$6 \cdot 49 = 294$	$7^3 = 343$	$\frac{294}{343} \approx 0.86$
8	$8^2 = 64$	$6 \cdot 64 = 384$	$8^3 = 512$	$\frac{384}{512} = 0.75$

c. The ratio gets smaller.

d.

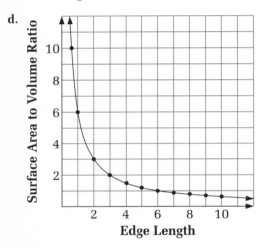

e. Answers may vary. An example is given. A similar relationship will exist between surface area and volume. **f.** Answers may vary. An example is given. whether the ice chest is made of plastic foam or regular plastic, whether the ice chest is insulated or not, thickness of sides, whether lid locks in place or just sits on top

Problem Set 10

1.a.

Percent Off	Number Sold
0%	70
5%	76
10%	82
15%	88
20%	94
25%	100
30%	106
35%	112
40%	118

b. 35% off or more **2.a.** 18 correct answers
b. 16 correct answers **3.a.** 5 min: Meilei 1500 m, grandfather 1250 m; n min: Meilei $300n$ m, grandfather $250n$ m **b.** Meilei $300(t - 1)$, grandfather $250t$
c. 6 min; 1500 m **4.** Let t = the total time (in hours). $6t + 14(t - 1) = 16$; $t = 1.5$ h **5.** any number less than 12;

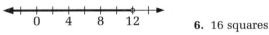

6. 16 squares

Problem Set 11

1.a. $2s + 3a = 18$ **b.** $a = -\frac{2}{3}s + 6$ **c.** 2 adult tickets **2.a.** $K = \frac{5}{9}R$ **b.** 491.67°R **c.** 373.15°K
3. 29 students **4.** roller coaster: 4 tickets; log flume: 3 tickets

Unifying Problem 5

a. Answers may vary. The value of z should be $\frac{1}{2}(x + y)$, and the value of h should be one half the height of $ABCD$. **b.** No. **c.** $\frac{1}{2}(x + y) \cdot 2h$; $\frac{1}{2}(y + z)h; \frac{1}{2}(x + z)h$
d. $\frac{1}{2}(x + y) \cdot 2h = \frac{1}{2}(y + z)h + \frac{1}{2}(x + z)h$
e. $z = \frac{1}{2}(x + y)$
f. No. There is no relationship between them.
g. The length of line segment EF is one half the sum of the lengths of the bases of the large trapezoid.

Problem Set 12

a. Answers may vary. Examples are given. First method: The number of households with no television set was 95,000,000 (0.02) or 1,900,000. So the number of households with one or more sets was 95,000,000 − 1,900,000 or 93,100,000.

Second method: 35% + 63% or 98% had at least one set. 95,000,000 (0.98) = 93,100,000.   **2.** about 60.2%
3.a. $\frac{4}{5}$ **b.** $\frac{1}{2}$ **c.** Yes. The more times an experiment is performed, the closer the experimental probability comes to the theoretical probability.   **4.** $2,400,000
5. 200 hits   **6.** about 17 bushels

Problem Set 13

1.a. 500 pigeons **b.** 125 pigeons   **c.** The first estimate was 4 times the second. Answers may vary. An example is given. the locations where the samples were collected, other birds that may have been in the vicinity when the samples were collected   **2.** $18\frac{3}{4}$ in.

3.a. 8 in. by 4 in.   **b.** No. $\frac{6}{10} \neq \frac{4}{8}$
c. Start with a square frame.   **4.** about 39,162 ft/min; about 445 mi/h

Unifying Problem 6

about 0.29

Problem Set 14

1.a. Answers may vary. An example is given.
$\frac{c}{y} = \frac{479.40}{12}$ **b.** 39.95   **c.** $799.00   **d.** Answers may vary. An example is given. color of carpet, thickness of carpet, whether you are buying enough to qualify for a discount   **2.** about 1002 ft

3.a.

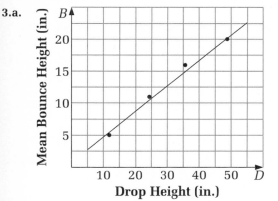

b–c. Answers may vary. Examples are given.
b. about 0.42; I used the points (35, 15) and (5, 2.5) and divided the vertical change by the horizontal change.   **c.** about 13 in.   **4.** 3 times   **5.** 11 trees

Problem Set 15

1.a. $d = 750h$; 1875 mi   **b.** $s = 20d$; 3 days
c. $c = 1.95s$; $29.25   **2.** 1638¢/h; $16.38/h
3.a. 3900 pesos   **b.** $1.60/gal   **4.** about 53 kg
5.a. 120°   **b.** about 105 cm²   **c.** $\frac{1}{3}, \frac{1}{3}, \frac{1}{3}$

Unifying Problem 7

1. radius = $\frac{1}{2}s$; circumference = πs; area = $\frac{1}{4}\pi s^2$

2. radius = $\frac{\sqrt{2}}{2}s$; circumference = $\sqrt{2}s\pi$;

area = $\frac{1}{2}\pi s^2$ **3.a.** $C_1 \approx 0.785\ P$ **b.** $C_2 \approx 1.11\ P$
c. $C_1 \approx 0.707\ C_2$ **d.** $A_1 \approx 0.785\ A_s$
e. $A_2 \approx 1.57\ A_s$ **f.** $A_1 = \frac{1}{2}A_2$ **4.** Draw a square whose corners are on the circle. Then draw a circle with a diameter the same length as a side of the square.

Problem Set 16

1.a. 400; 392; 384; 360; 320; 240

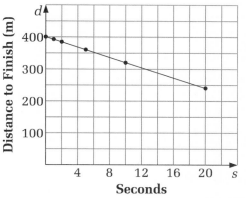

b. slope: −8, vertical intercept: 400; The slope is the rate at which he is approaching the finish line. The vertical intercept is his distance from the finish line at the beginning of the race.   **c.** 50 seconds after the race begins; horizontal intercept   **d.** $d = 400 - 8s$
e. $0 \le s \le 50$ **2.a.** 6 envelopes; 5 envelopes
b. $6j + 5f = 600$

c.

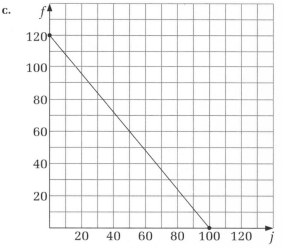

d. The horizontal intercept is 100, the vertical intercept is 120. 100 min is the time it would take for Jolene to do the job working alone; 120 min is the time it would take Frank working alone.   **3.** $c = 100$; 0
4.a. a vertical line; $x = -2$ **b.** No. Using any two points, slope = $\frac{\text{change in } y}{0}$, and division by 0 is undefined.

Problem Set 17

1.a. control: age, dependent: weight
b. (2, 28), (5, 40)   **c.** 4 lb per year
d. $w = 4a + 20$ $(1 \leq a \leq 7)$ **2.a.** $s = -10d + 92$
b. 92   **3.a.** $y = 0.3x + 5$ **b.** $y = 0.5x$
c. The solution is (25, 12.5).

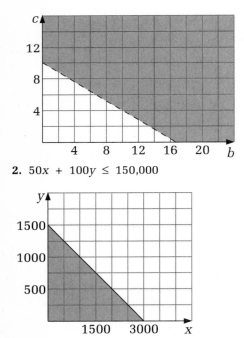

d. the point where the total expenses is the same as the income from selling the brownies   **e.** (25, 12.5)
f. Answers may vary. An example is given. If the group sells the brownies for $.80 each, then they will have to sell 10 brownies to break even.

Problem Set 18

1.a. $5c + 3b$
b. $5c + 3b > 50$

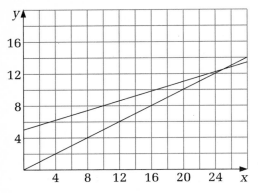

2. $50x + 100y \leq 150,000$

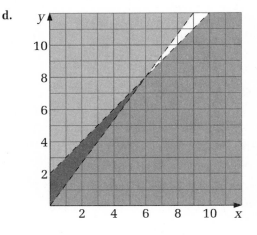

3.a. $1.5w + 5t \leq 200$ **b.** $w + t \geq 50$
c.

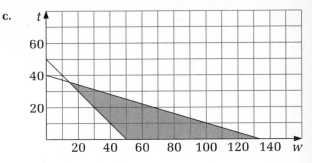

130 workbooks and 1 textbook

4.a. $100x = 75y$ **b.** $100x < 75y$ **c.** $y < x + 2$
d.

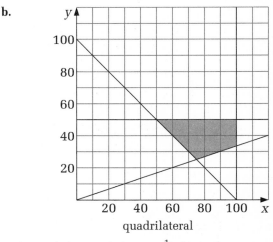

Unifying Problem 8

Answers may vary, depending on how variables are chosen (which for peanuts, which for cashews, which for the horizontal axis and which for the vertical axis). Examples are given.   **a.** Let x = pounds of peanuts, y = pounds of cashews.
$x + y \geq 100, x \leq 3y, 0 \leq x \leq 100, 0 \leq y \leq 50$

b.

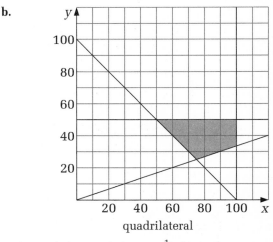

quadrilateral

c. (50, 50), (100, 50), (100, $33\frac{1}{3}$), (75, 25)

d. $c = 1.79x + 3.99y$ **e.** 75 lb peanuts, 25 lb cashews; $234

Problem Set 19

1. about 103 in.   **2.** $2\sqrt{41}$ mi   **3.** If I date a girl, then she goes to West High. If a girl goes to West High, then I date her. probably not true   **4.** No. Yes. Each wall is square with the floor, since $1^2 + 1^2 = 2 \approx (1.41)^2$. The walls are not square with each other, since $1^2 + 1^2 = 2 \neq (1.35)^2$.

Problem Set 20

1. about 0.14 (assuming no two planes are in the air at the same time)   **2.** red: 30°, green: 270°, blue: 60°
3. They should choose the pyramid roof. about 144 ft²
4. about 1237 cm³

Problem Set 21

1. square pyramid   **2.** a factor of 25; 875 in.²
3.a. 2400 ft   **b.** 1,200,000 ft³   **c.** 9,600,000 ft³

Unifying Problem 9

1.a. $a = \sqrt{2}, b = 2, c = 2\sqrt{2}, d = 4$ **b.** Each square has sides that are $\sqrt{2}$ times the length of a side of the previous square.   **c.** $4\sqrt{2}$ **d.** 1, 2, 4, 8, 16
e. Each square has an area that is two times the area of the previous square.   **f.** 32   **2.a.** $\sqrt{3}$ **b.** 3
c. $3\sqrt{3}, 9, 9\sqrt{3}$

Problem Set 22

1. an isosceles triangle; the altitude from the vertex where the sides of equal length intersect   **2.a.** the line with equation $y = 0$, that is, the x-axis   **b.** the line with equation $x = -4.5$ **3.a.** not if there is a line that goes through all three points   **b.** No. The points all lie on the line with equation $y = 7$.
4.a. $y = (x + 2)(x - 4)$ **b.** Graphs may vary, but should resemble the graph shown in Problem 4 and should pass through $(-2, 0), (0, -8)$, and $(4, 0)$. Yes.

Problem Set 23

1.a. Diedre; Matt found $x^2 \cdot x^3$ instead of $(x^2)^3$.
b. Matt; Diedre did not square the factor 3.   **c.** Matt; Diedre did not find the fifth power of -1 correctly.
2.a. $27r^3$ **b.** $9r (12r)(6r)$ or $648r^3$ **c.** 24 boxes
3.a. $3s^2 + 6s$ **b.** $3s(s + 2)$; Yes, provided you group the factors 3 and s for one of the dimensions.
4.a. $y = (x - 3)(x - 5)$ **b.** $y = (x + 1)(x - 4)$
c. $y = (x + 10)(x + 20)$ **5.** No. Counterexamples may vary. An example is given.
$(x + 2)(x - 2) = x^2 - 4$, which is not a trinomial.

Problem Set 24

1.a.

Factor	1	2	3	4	6	8	12	24
Factor	−24	−12	−8	−6	−4	−3	−2	−1

b. No. There are still eight combinations: 1 and 24, 2 and 12, 3 and 8, 4 and 6, −1 and −24, −2 and −12, −3 and −8, and −4 and −6.   **2.** D; The horizontal intercepts are at −1 and −2.   **3.** C; The horizontal intercepts are at −1 and 2.
4. B; $x^2 + x - 2 = (x + 2)(x - 1)$, so the horizontal intercepts are at −2 and 1.   **5.** A; $x^2 - 3x + 2 = (x - 2)(x - 1)$, so the horizontal intercepts are at 1 and 2.   **6.a.** 100; The rocket is 100 m above ground level before it is launched.
b. about −2.47 and 8.25; −2.47 is irrelevant. The model rocket will reach the ground in about 8.25 s.
c. about 141 m

Unifying Problem 10

1.a–f.

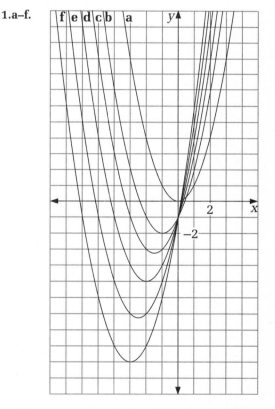

g. The vertex moves left and down.   **h.** The vertex will move right and down.   **2.** Yes. Express the trinomial on the right side of the equation in the form $(x + a)^2 + b$. The graph of $y = (x + a)^2 + b$ is the graph of $y = x^2$ translated $|a|$ units left or right, $|b|$ units up or down.
